W9-CUI-774

From Princeton/Masters

This 112 page book is a special abridged edition of the latest book by one of America's leading authorities on job and career change. The full 336 page edition is available at finer bookstores. Originally entitled The Professional Job Changing System, the previous editions have sold more than 1,500,000 copies, and have received universal praise in hundreds of media. A sampling of reviewer comments on previous editions is listed below.

"An indispensable aid."   **Business Week**

"A complete source of professional knowledge."
                                            Personnel Journal

"The best handbook for finding a better job!"
                                              Chicago Today

"Honest-to-God this tells you how to get a better job!"
                          Training in Business & Industry

"Capable of catapulting almost any person!"
                                            Purchasing Week

"Highly recommended!"   **Vocational Guidance Quarterly**

"Amazingly readable."   **Memphis Press-Scimitar**

"Excellent. A good investment."   **Nation's Business**

"Hundreds of new ideas for people!"   **Houston Chronicle**

"Inside information!"   **St. Paul Pioneer Press**

"The latest job hunting concepts."   **San Bernardino Sun**

Library of Congress Catalog Card Number 93-83798

ISBN 1-882885-03-1 (pocket size paper)

Attention Schools and Businesses: Books by Princeton/ Masters Press are available at quantity discounts. For information, write: Princeton/Masters Press Inc., 7951 E. Maplewood, Suite 333, Englewood, CO, 80111 or call 800-772-4446.

An Easier Way to Change Jobs

A Condensed Version of
The Princeton/Masters
Job Changing System

By Bob Gerberg

About the author

Bob Gerberg has a BA degree from Colgate University and an MBA degree from the University of Pittsburgh. His successful career has included positions as a VP of Marketing and Assistant to the Chairman of a Fortune 500 company. A leading authority in the career and outplacement field, he has authored more than two dozen books, publications and cassettes on job and career change.

About Princeton Masters

Princeton/Masters is an outplacement firm with offices and associates in major cities. The firm offers a wide range of books, cassette programs, courses and private marketing programs, which include professional writing assistance, database research, printing and mailing services and the management of job campaigns.

The firm works for employers who are outplacing or relocating their staffs and individuals who retain the firm on a private basis.

Contents

If you use old methods...
job hunting can take a long time!

Listed below is a chart developed from a survey of more than 4,000 professionals, managers and executives. The data represents the estimated average job search for out-of-work executives in 1993-94.

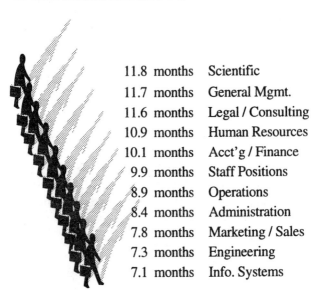

11.8 months	Scientific
11.7 months	General Mgmt.
11.6 months	Legal / Consulting
10.9 months	Human Resources
10.1 months	Acct'g / Finance
9.9 months	Staff Positions
8.9 months	Operations
8.4 months	Administration
7.8 months	Marketing / Sales
7.3 months	Engineering
7.1 months	Info. Systems

This system is easier, faster… and far more effective

With America's current economic position in the world, the number of *attractive jobs* with major employers has been expanding at a slow rate. In addition, a half million new college graduates are entering the market each year, the percentage of women seeking employment continues to expand, and people are living and working longer.

Up until now, most people have allowed their lives to be determined by jobs that simply come their way. Typically, people engage in *"passive"* job hunting by waiting for ads to appear, for recruiters to call, or for contacts to give them a call about an opening.

As a result, millions settle for less and are underemployed, simply because of their dependence on traditional job hunting methods. However, as you will appreciate from this system, the revolution in personal computers, databases and other sources for information can make job hunting a much easier and faster experience.

This system will give you a more scientific approach to maximizing every job hunting action you take. It also emphasizes new and well-organized approaches for going to your markets, and for uncovering many new options. We call it *"pro-active"* rather than *"passive"* job hunting. The object is to help cut your job hunting time in half, perhaps more, and to help you produce better results as well.

Never fall victim to these common job hunting myths

Famous Last Words

"Sending out a lot of resumes is all I need."

"I can always get a job with my contacts."

"Answering ads is the key for me."

"Recruiters will always be after someone like me."

"If I get the interview… I'll get the job."

"My friends say I have a great resume."

And…Famous Last Excuses

"The economy is so bad. There are no jobs out there."

"My field is slow, and it's impossible to change careers."

"I just don't have the right leads or contacts."

Chapter 1— Marketability

The starting point with our system is to raise your marketability and income potential. Here are some tips!

Job hunting is about how you give yourself a competitive edge. Never limit your thinking, and make yourself as marketable as possible.

See if your real knowledge can make you more marketable

Now, it has been said time and again by psychologists, motivational speakers, spiritual leaders and coaches, that the most restrictive limits you face are those you put on yourself. So, if you really want to be a serious candidate for a better position, don't put any limits on your thinking and be willing to go for it!

When it comes to job hunting, what everyone thinks of first is experience. However, most of us think of our experience in more narrow terms than we should. That type of thinking restricts our opportunities as many good situations pass by unnoticed.

As you go through this chapter, we will review a number of ways that will enable you to take a new view of your total experience and how you can describe it to potential employers.

To begin with, make a list of things you know. For example, knowledge of a job, a product, a process or a market? It could come from work, hobbies, schooling, reading, activities or from suppliers, customers, friends or your social life. Whatever that knowledge, you may be able to use it to improve your marketability.

Remember—your personality and other factors are also marketable

Personality, of course, is just a word for that mysterious combination of traits that can either attract us to someone quite strongly, or on the other hand, leave us unimpressed.

Many employment decisions are based on personality. It happens every day. For example, *"He's certainly a positive, quick-thinking fellow. I like him, and better yet, I trust him. He'll be able to get along with our people and provide leadership. I want him in this company, and I'm going to make an offer right now."*

If some aspect of your personality makes you suited for certain types of activities, look into whether it can lead to a preferred career direction. Also, don't ever forget that your character is marketable. Qualities of integrity, thoughtfulness and loyalty count! Your interests and enthusiasm are also marketable. How many employers have hired people because they showed a great interest in their business? The answer is, a lot!

Doing this exercise can help expand your marketability

List "any experience you've had" in a way that makes the experience more transferrable.

First, list your experience by your transferrable skills and/or your duties that are commonly performed in almost all companies, e.g. analyzing, organizing, project management, group skills and problem solving.

Second, list your experience according to "business functions" that apply to most businesses, such as sales, production, accounting, market research, purchasing, etc.

Third, list your experience by using "action verbs" that describe what you did and that translate those things into achievements. For example, controlled, scheduled, systematized, etc. *The more ways you describe your experience, the more they can qualify you for jobs in many career fields and industries.*

Use "phrases" that employers want to hear — and your marketability will expand

Our philosophy revolves around identifying the "core" words and phrases that you will always be ready to use... *words* that communicate your special strengths. They should become a regular part of *"your story"* for employers, recruiters and others.

Your "tickets alone" (degrees, lofty titles, etc.) will not necessarily motivate an employer to hire you. Those credentials only offer one form of reassurance that suggests you are right for the job.

This is why you must use words that add interest beyond your credentials. For example, words such as adaptable, analytic, competitive, decisive, enthusiastic, imaginative, open-minded, perceptive, productive, sincere, tactful, versatile, etc. When employers recruit people, they usually have phrases like these in mind that describe the person they are looking to hire.

perseverence —
dedicated
honest
trustworthy —
motivated —
ambitious —

team player

Decide on phrases that relate to you, and select those that set you apart. For example, you may have *"operated effectively under pressure."* Perhaps you are *"an excellent motivator,"* or you may have *"built a highly effective team."* One of your strengths may be that you are *"a good listener"* or someone who can *"work well with all types of people."*

At Princeton/Masters we use our *Career History and Marketability Profile* to help people uncover what's marketable about them. This profile contains a list of all the phrases that employers commonly seek. On your own, you need to make a list of at least twenty key phrases that describe you, and that set you apart from others.

> I am an action person... a problem solver... a skillful negotiator... I can get things done... I am a "team player."

If you broaden your "career" options— your marketability will soar

Every month people start new careers or enter frontier industries, areas where they have no previous experience.

Chances are, there are new careers and industries, as well as advanced opportunities within your field, that will be worth your examination. While *The Dictionary of Occupational Titles* lists 22,000 different jobs, 95% of all job opportunities fall within 300 career specialties.

At Princeton/Masters, we've found that most people can select between five and fifteen of these options as possibilities for themselves.

Today, people can also change industries on an easier basis than ever before. Remember, long term success has a lot to do with being in the right industry at the right time. Organizations in fast growing industries cannot find enough people with knowledge of their field, so they are forced to go outside to recruit people with the best natural talent they can find.

If you were to go through a checklist of the 1,600 traditional industries and the 300 fastest growing ones, you would probably uncover 15 to 25 different industries where you are marketable.

You will also be more marketable if you contact small business

Over the last decade, America's largest 2,000 companies have been reducing employment. While they have many opportunities that become available because of turnover, the majority of new jobs are available with small to medium sized organizations. However, you will need to take advantage of several databases to find the ones that might be right for you *(see chapter 3)*.

In San Francisco / Oakland

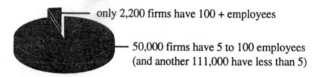

only 2,200 firms have 100 + employees

50,000 firms have 5 to 100 employees
(and another 111,000 have less than 5)

In Houston

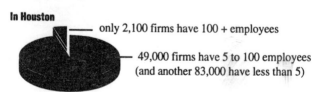

only 2,100 firms have 100 + employees

49,000 firms have 5 to 100 employees
(and another 83,000 have less than 5)

In Denver / Boulder

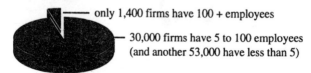

only 1,400 firms have 100 + employees

30,000 firms have 5 to 100 employees
(and another 53,000 have less than 5)

" About Finding the
Great American Job. . .
The Rules of the Game
Have Changed Forever. "

From the Cover of
Time Magazine, Nov. 22, 1993

The seven primary ways
for getting interviews

The chapters that follow cover the
seven primary ways for getting the right interviews.

- ❑ Events & unadvertised jobs
- ❑ Direct mail
- ❑ Contacting recruiters
- ❑ Telemarketing
- ❑ Networking
- ❑ Creating a job
- ❑ Answering ads

12% Published

88% Unpublished

The Job Market

Chapter 2— Unadvertised Jobs

Our system has people focus on the 88% of all jobs that are not advertised. Here's one direct way to find them!

News of these events are the key
to finding unadvertised openings

- ❑ new products
- ❑ firms relocating
- ❑ new leases
- ❑ higher sales & profits
- ❑ new officers
- ❑ planned expansions

Most jobs are filled by referrals, from resumes on file, or through people who contact firms at the right time.

Many studies have indicated that about 88% of all openings are filled privately. How do companies do this? Well, they seek to fill openings privately by looking first within their own companies. They may also review any resumes they've kept on file. But in most cases, they ultimately fill positions through referrals or by hiring someone who contacts them at the right time.

Now, if you can learn where these openings exist, it stands to reason that you can have a major edge. What's more, you might be able to have your credentials up for singular consideration, instead of applying right along with scores of others.

To find unadvertised openings just read the business press

You can uncover jobs which are not advertised through mailings, telemarketing and networking, but the most direct way is simple. Events occur every day in thousands of firms that ultimately lead managers to begin the process of privately looking for new people.

These events are often reported in local and national business publications, trade magazines, newsletters and newspapers, e.g. growth situations, new divisions, new facilities, new products, reorganizations, acquisitions, executive changes, and plans for expansion.

For companies undergoing these transitions, chances are they will need to attract people to handle problems or capitalize on opportunities. The activity in these companies won't usually be limited. They can be expected to need people in all functional categories.

While private openings are being filled by all types of employers, they are filled with far greater frequency in organizations experiencing significant change.

When you read about a company that is giving out signals that they may be hiring at an above-average rate, don't stop at the obvious implications. Use what we refer to as *"ripple-effect thinking."* This is simply taking the time to think about all of the changes that may be occurring — up and down the line and across many functions.

You may also get some ideas about using information you read about one company— to find opportunities with their suppliers, customers or even their competitors.

At Princeton/Masters we believe that news events which signal emerging opportunities are so important that our research department provides a specialized service for our clients. For a given metropolitan area we track these situations, and compile them in our computers. In many cases the reports we supply have enabled people to move with great speed in contacting the right organizations and securing new jobs *(see pages 102-103)*.

In summary, it's been often said that information is power, and that's exactly what emerging opportunities provide. The ability to recognize and go after opportunity has been critical to the success of many people. It is especially important for those who want to change careers or industries.

How a few people have capitalized on private openings

❑ A financial executive learned that a troubled manufacturer was divesting a division to raise cash. He called the new president and arranged to meet him and explain how he might help. Four weeks later he became the CFO of this company.

❑ A homemaker learned that a major firm was establishing a warehouse in the next town. She phoned to learn the name of the person responsible and was the first administrator hired.

❑ A marketing manager read that a European corporation had bought a local company. He wrote to express interest and suggested a dialogue when European officials visited there. Twelve weeks later, he was VP-Marketing, U.S.A. at $120,000.

Chapter 3— Direct Mail

A fast way for getting interviews—
but you must have the right list and
materials. A key part of our system,
here are some rules that work.

Direct mail works! But,
you need the right databases
to quickly find the right contacts.

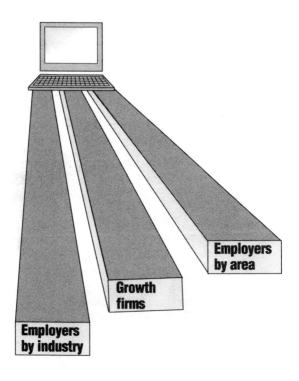

To make direct mail work, you need superior resumes and letters along with the right selection of people to contact. Your *"contact list"* needs to be set by (1) the industries you prefer; and (2) your preferred metro areas.

The people you will want to contact should be a level or two above where you want to be. Senior VPs in charge of functions are recommended for most people. In smaller firms you need to reach the top executives or owners.

To assemble your list you will want to access computer databases to save both time and money. At Princeton/ Masters we maintain virtually every major database of value to job hunters, and we do so on a current basis. Then, our clients give us their criteria (*industries & metro areas*), and we can get them a customized computer report on their full contact list on an overnight basis.

This full list can be 200, 500 or 3,500 employers— depending on the criteria. Then, divide your list into three parts: e.g. (1) your "best of best;" (2) other prime choices; and (3) secondary choices.

(If you have a friend with access to the major databases on employers throughout the United States, now is the time to ask for a favor.)

For best results, follow these direct mail rules

Direct mail marketing is a separate marketing specialty. What works and what doesn't has already been proven!

❑ Don't mention income and don't try to explain "why" you are looking. Long copy and long letters work!

❑ Keep sentences short. Avoid flowery words. Keep paragraphs to five or six lines. Indent the first line. Sign your name with a blue felt tip pen. It implies forcefulness. If you write a handwritten P.S., it will almost always be read, so make the copy good.

❑ Never begin a letter by asking for a job. Stress career orientation. Never hard sell... *"If this guy is so good, why does he try so hard?"*

❑ When writing to a stranger say you have some "ideas" or "knowledge" that can benefit the firm. Then, offer to share the knowledge in a meeting. If you have industry experience, mention it early! There is nothing quite like an industry hook.

❑ Persuasive letters are alive and enthusiastic, as well as personal and warm. They "read" just like you "speak." Read a letter out loud. If you find you are changing parts as you read, it needs more work.

❑ Personalize your correspondence. Use the names of the firm and the individual in the body of your letter.

❏ Pay careful attention to editing. Eliminating extraneous information makes important facts stand out.

❏ Making use of a third party can be very effective. Offer to prepare a letter for their signature and be sure they are knowledgeable about your situation.

❏ Commit yourself to a telephone follow-up. Name the date and general time when you will call. Also, after every interview write a follow-up letter. Show enthusiasm for the company and/or the position.

❏ The best day to mail is Sunday. The time to reach people is from Tuesday to Thursday. Avoid mailings between Thanksgiving and Christmas. Summer mailings also yield less than average.

❏ Keep exact records of all of your direct mail, and keep everything you receive back—including rejections. Follow-up mailings get 80% of the response generated from your first mailing.

❏ Telegrams are always read. Faxing unasked-for resumes is a waste of time.

❏ If you have a strong interest in a particular employer, consider sending materials to several individuals in a large organization.

Remember—success will depend on your list, your materials and your follow-up

Let's assume you were seeking a sales manager's position. Here are some direct mail actions to consider.

1—High risk

Sent to firms and by generic titles, e.g., all VPs of Sales at Fortune 500 firms. Takes great credentials to work.

2—Much better

Sent to VP of Sales, by name, selected by industry, size and location. Works best with telephone follow-up.

3—Very good

Sent to VP of Sales by name; in industries where you have experience, mention it early, and follow up.

4—Excellent

Sent to VP of Sales you have spoken to first on the phone. Great if you can get your telemarketing going.

5—Also Excellent

Sent to VP Sales, by name, where mailing goes out under someone else's letterhead and title.

6—Outstanding

Sent to VP Sales, to whom you've been referred by someone you can mention, with telephone follow-up.

7—Best

Sent to VP Sales, that you have previously met, either social or business, with telephone follow-up.

Chapter 4—Recruiters

Recruiters control 9% of the market. Here's how to find the right ones and make the right contact.

Jan, this is Bill Smith. Would you be interested in confidentially exploring something new?

There are more than 5,000 recruiting firms with more than 30,000 professionals in the U.S. The key is to contact the right ones for you—and to do it with the right material!

Recruiters have a preference for persons who are achievers, who make a strong first impression and who are successfully employed in other firms. These are the individuals who are most presentable to their clients.

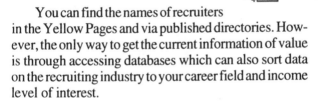

To initiate contact with recruiters you are going to have to send them a superior summary of your qualifications. At an executive level, you may need to do mailings of 300 or more. A second mailing to the same list three months later usually produces equal results.

You can find the names of recruiters in the Yellow Pages and via published directories. However, the only way to get the current information of value is through accessing databases which can also sort data on the recruiting industry to your career field and income level of interest.

Princeton /Masters maintains information covering all recruiters of significance. This includes thousands of firms who are active in every career field. We make available custom computer reports with names, addresses and specialties sorted by your income needs, career field and by your preferred metro areas and/or region *(see pages 102-103)*.

The types of professional recruiters today

Executive search firms typically fill positions at $60,000 to $250,000 and up. Many people refer to them as headhunters. Their assignment is to find candidates who meet specialized criteria. They are retained for searches on an exclusive basis, and most charge their employer clients 30% to 33% of annual compensation. They are also sometimes referred to as "retainer recruiters."

Professional agencies are also known as headhunters. These mid-level recruiters usually concentrate on finding people between $30,000 and $85,000 per year and are not normally retained on an exclusive basis. Many specialize by industry or career function, and are sometimes referred to as "contingency recruiters," in that they only get paid if they fill the position.

Many of these professionals can be valuable career allies to professionals and managers. They know what's going on in their local market.

A key point to remember is that whether they are called search firms, recruiters, headhunters or agencies, all of the firms in these categories work for (and are paid by) employers. Their function is to locate, screen and recommend prospective employees.

Executive search firms currently account for fewer than 5,000 placements per month on a national scale. Furthermore, fewer than a dozen firms control most of the business, even though there are upwards of 600 organizations who claim to be in that segment of the business.

Certain recruiters enjoy considerable prestige, often working only on select high-level assignments. However, there are also many fine smaller firms who specialize by industries or disciplines. The mid-level recruiters have been playing an increasingly important role in the job market.

Besides specializing by industry, many of these firms specialize in accounting, data processing or sales, and while some are national franchise organizations, there are many local firms which can be helpful to you.

For the most part, recruiters are articulate professionals who have a broad knowledge of business. It will pay you to develop relationships with those you respect.

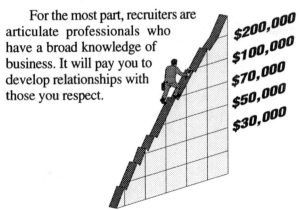

$200,000
$100,000
$70,000
$50,000
$30,000

Keep these tips in mind about contacting recruiters

❏ Get to know as many as you can before you need them. Be honest while pursuing a soft sell. If you are desperate or too available, they will never recommend you to their clients.

❏ Your chances of reaching recruiters when they have an assignment for your background may be slim, and career changers can't expect much here.

❏ Keep in mind that recruiters are focused on their active contracts and have only secondary interest in people who contact them from other specialties. Because large firms are contacted by 50 to 200 job seekers each day, there may be instances where a recruiter calls you *months* later.

❏ The best relationships are the ones that begin with recruiters contacting you. Being visible in your industry is the major key to success with recruiters. Being in a hot field or industry can improve things still further.

❏ In summary, recruiters can be very important and you should develop some interviews through them. However, no more than 10% of your job hunting efforts should be directed toward recruiters.

Chapter 5— Telemarketing

By working with the right databases
and scripts, telemarketing can be
a fast way to get interviews.

Setting interviews over
the phone is a lot
easier than you
think!

Effective use of the phone is easier than you think. Of course, some people are totally confident in their ability to use the phone. However, 90% of all job seekers are reluctant to pick up the phone and make a "cold call."

If you're not experienced in using the phone, believe it or not, it's a mostly friendly and helpful world out there. Most people at all levels are courteous and polite and go out of their way to project a good image for their company.

Still, there is a certain misconception that all secretaries and assistants will always keep you from speaking with their bosses. They do screen calls, but it is part of their job to make sure that contact is made when appropriate.

The difference between making simply phone calls and "telemarketing" is very basic. When you telemarket you have specific goals and you use a standardized procedure for making a large number of calls.

To do aggressive telemarketing and to make the process easy, you will need to be able to access employer databases. It's essential to have all the information you need right at your fingertips. What's more, you need it organized in a manner that facilitates your making large numbers of calls within a very short time period. Being organized will also make your follow-up easy.

Ideally, you should put your full database on "organizer software." Then you could even have your computer dial for you, automatically put out your follow-up letter, and remind you when it is time to call again.

Proven telemarketing guidelines that work

Get used to making one call after another. Stand up and you'll give a power assist to your voice. Be prepared for rejection. Effective use of the phone is a numbers game. You can easily make 15 calls an hour.

❏

Do your phone work in batches, and you will need only one success each time to sustain your morale. To warm up, use some throw-away calls to get yourself started.

❏

Make sure you know how you will be answering your phone. List questions you may be asked and write out the answers to the difficult ones.

❏

You should also prepare 30-second and 60-second commercials of your most important selling points. Rehearse it. Tape it and critique it. Your effort will pay off.

❏

Call executives before 9:00 a.m. or after 5:00 p.m. when they may answer their own phone.

❏

Project a natural, confident tone— as you would when talking with a friend. Lower your voice. Speak slowly and don't give the impression you're rushed.

Smile while speaking over the phone and your voice will sound more pleasant.

❏

Be friendly, enthusiastic and if you encounter objections stay friendly, but sometimes answer a question with a question. Be sure your phone is answered properly. No clever answering machine messages!

❏

The secretary doesn't really know who you are or your purpose. If you retain the thought that you only want advice and information, the decision maker has no reason to shy away from you. When speaking with the secretary, get her name and use it. Be confident, positive and polite.

❏

When following up, do not discuss your business other than to say the executive is expecting your call. Or, use your job title to get by the secretary.

❏

If you begin to generate interest, do not reveal too much of your story. Never be interviewed on the phone.

Approaches for opening your conversations

The good news approach

"Mr. Ellis: When I heard about your four quarters of record growth ..." Everyone likes to have good things happen and to hear from others who are enthusiastic about their good fortune.

The third-party approach

Mention the name of a third party who knows the person you're calling. It establishes rapport, and also works when people don't know each other. *"Bill Regan, a partner with Arthur Andersen, thought I should get in touch with you. He felt your growth suggests a good employment possibility. Do you have a moment?"*

The specific reason approach

"Mr. Franklin, I have a specific reason for calling you. I know the line of business you are in and something of the processes you use. During the past 15 months, I have been able to save a company like yours approximately $850,000. I would like to share the details with you. Does your calendar permit a meeting later this week?"

Tips for handling people who screen your call

❏ Use the name of the person who is the "screener." Once identified, they will become more personal. If possible, identify yourself with an organization.

❏ If you don't get through on your first attempt, suggest a time when you will call the screener back. Don't leave messages.

❏ Consider reversing your attempt to speak with the decision maker by asking for a referral to another line manager in the area in which you might want to work.

❏ Ask two or three penetrating questions about the company's needs. When asked such questions, people are inclined to refer you to an appropriate line manager.

❏ After a few days, you can also call back the screener and explain that while the personnel people were helpful, they were not really able to answer your questions.

❏ You may encounter the question: *"Are you looking for a job?"* The answer might be: *"Yes, I am; do you think you could help me? Although I'm employed, a friend suggested your firm to me."*

❏ Or, you may encounter the comment, *"We don't have any openings at the present time."* The response: *"I appreciate a person who is direct; however, I have such a strong interest in the firm, I really believe that I could be a great asset. Will you allow me to tell you why?"*

"We'd like to honor you for being the only job hunter to get through every barrier... and reach our boss."

Chapter 6— Networking

Our system uses a focused-industry type of networking. Start with the right databases, and it will be easy to expand your contacts.

Networking —
getting others to:

- ❏ act as a reference
- ❏ suggest referrals
- ❏ contact employers
- ❏ recommend recruiters
- ❏ supply information
- ❏ make introductions

"I was with a friend of mine today and I'm bringing him in to head up our new operations."

Your network may include former employers, suppliers, ministers, alumni, social contacts, insurance agents, bankers, merchants, relatives, teachers, trade association officers, attorneys, clients, etc.

To network effectively will require that you capitalize on the name of one individual to gain an interview with another. For example, every time you meet with a firm, if you feel that the interview would not be productive, be sure to lead into a discussion about another firm. Then, ask your interviewer whether or not he felt that it would be a good firm for you to explore.

He's likely to routinely say, *"Of course, you ought to contact them."* Your next step would be to write the president of the new firm something like the following, *"In my recent meeting with Mr. X, he suggested that it might be of value if I arranged to speak with you."*

There is a big difference between focused networking, which is targeted by industry or involves influentials, and universal networking, which may be purely social or for advice purposes. The latter can take a long time.

At Princeton/Masters we take advantage of databases to identify the people in the right industries that our clients should consider networking. We also use them to identify influential people who can be of general help.

Networking—
through influential people

Governors, congressional representatives, state senators and politicians at almost any level can be excellent sources for referrals. The same is true for prominent doctors and lawyers who speak with many people during the course of each day.

Clergy, accountants, hospital trustees, members of the Chamber of Commerce or other civic groups, members of industrial development boards, investment bankers, insurance brokers, and many others also fall into this category.

Expand your business network by attending seminars and supplier meetings. Make yourself visible. Take an active role in community affairs, politics, and service clubs. Trade shows can be an efficient medium for developing contacts. In one location you usually have dozens of people assembled, and all of them are there because they want to talk to people.

The executive directors of associations, Chambers of Commerce, and fraternal organizations such as the Toastmasters usually have many "lines" into their communities. They know where growth is occurring.

Professional groups also manage business magazines, journals, newsletters, industry directories, trade show catalogs and many other publications. The editors at these journals can be influential contacts.

"I've gathered the top 1% of
my network here."

You can also network from a *"zero"* base. A technique for doing this is commonly called the *"insider approach."* For example, call a salesperson and ask, *"Is there a chance you could help me?"* Then ask the person to spend a few minutes to give you an estimate of your chances for getting into the firm. It's easy to get a third-party introduction to a person.

If you are at a junior level or seeking your first civilian job, you may wish to encourage suggestions from senior executives concerning the direction of your career. You could write executives with whom you are not acquainted. Of course, your *"advice letter"* would have to be well phrased. You must convey your respect for their expertise on these matters in an appealing way.

The object of this approach is to have them take more than a passing interest in your success. Your goal would be to obtain job leads in either the firms of these executives or those of their associates.

Consider these networking tips

There are many common errors that people make while networking. Here are some points worth remembering.

❑   Getting through to people and making arrangements to see them isn't the victory. That comes only after you've completed a successful interview.

❑   Do your homework and be prepared. Know what you want to say and practice it first. Decide what strengths or achievements you want to get across.

❑   Leave every meeting with more new names, and of course, always remember the names of secretaries.

❑   Networking is part of the "job" of looking for a job. List the people you might want to get to see. Then, find a way to get someone to help you to them.

❑ Use your network right the first time around. They may also be needed in the future. Talk with people wherever you go—work, church, professional association meetings, casual get-togethers. Let people know that you are thinking about a new opportunity.

❑ If you are likely to forget your questions, try keeping them in a notebook. Remember to keep your interviews brief. Ask for 15-minute appointments.

❑ Most people today know when they're "being networked." That doesn't mean they won't help you. It only means you shouldn't try to fool them.

❑ Send a handwritten thank-you note after interviews.

❑ Keep a file of all business cards. Follow every lead. Making advance judgment calls about a contact prior to a thorough investigation may short-circuit the networking process.

❑ Remember, networking is a proven way to search for a new job. Whenever you don't have other actions to take, you should be expanding your contacts.

When you network, ask the right questions

❏ *What are some important trends affecting your industry?*

❏ *What skills are companies looking for in new people?*

❏ *What are some good sources of added information—or people to talk to?*

❏ *Who are the recruiters active in the industry?*

❏ *In this business, are there any areas that offer faster than average opportunities for promotion?*

❏ *From what you know of my career up to now, what would be the logical next step?*

❏ *Do my qualifications contain any gaps that I should expand on?*

❏ *Could you refer me to any other people who know about these positions?*

❏ *The ultimate question, of course, is "Do you know anyone who might be interested in seeing me?"*

Chapter 7— Creating A Job

You can get employers to create a job— even when no opening exists!

This is a good approach for those who want a job tailored to their abilities

This approach can work for people with specialized talents or value. For example, a technical person who can develop new products for a company, a sales executive with contacts in particular markets, or a general manager who can start up a division in a specific industry.

The *"create a job"* approach should also be considered by anyone who may have difficulty winning offers through other means.

This includes those who have a narrow market for their talents; people who wish to change industries; those who have been unemployed for a while or who want to stay in a specific geographic or industry area.

I like you Jones. I want you to talk to my V.P. about a new project I have in mind for you.

In these situations, to win the job you want, you may have to create it by making an employer aware of your ability to make contributions.

You may fall into one or the other category, someone who *"needs to"* use this approach, or someone who simply *"wants to"* take advantage of its potential.

Regardless, keep in mind this simple thought. Employers hire people whenever they are persuaded that the benefit of having the person on board sufficiently outweighs the dollar cost. The following pages will give you some guiding principles to help make this approach work.

For the most part your goal should be to reach high level people in small to medium sized firms. This includes firms that are growing rapidly, bringing out new products, forming new divisions, acquiring other companies or reorganizing. These companies need good people, often from other industries. They are free to make decisive moves quickly. Large corporations are the least likely to respond.

Get across your benefit proposition

Another principle is to make sure that you get across your benefit proposition. It must be an accurate, concise and easily understood description of what you can do. It has to hold the promise of tangible value on a scale large enough to warrant an investment in you. In that initial communication, you need to establish your credentials. Mention specific results you achieved in the past. They are the best indicators of what you can do in the future.

Achievements you cite don't have to be large, but they do have to be significant. For instance, if you are an office manager, you might state that you managed a smooth introduction of new systems that lifted staff productivity by 40%.

One of two keys to remember is that if you have an exciting idea to communicate, it may help if you can show how someone else has already used that idea successfully.

Dealing with opportunities is a key job for many executives. Most don't have enough time in the day, and they are predisposed to positive news from people who can help them. They will want to believe your message, so all you need do is make sure you provide positive reinforcement.

Take strong initiatives

There are three things you need to accomplish in your first meeting. They are (1) learning what the employer really wants; (2) building your rapport; and (3) stirring their imagination.

Your first goal is to find out the employer's views. What does he see as the key challenges? What is the "hot button"? Where are the priorities? What attempts were made in the past?

Most important, try to get the employer to share his innermost thoughts. Try to find out his vision for the organization. Only when he starts to think about this and the achievements he might realize, would he consider creating a job.

Reinforce your value by drawing a clear picture of the benefits you can bring. Build enough enthusiasm to be asked to speak with others or be brought back for a second interview.

If you're not succeeding, try the "report option"

Here, you need to make an offer to study the situation in more detail, perhaps to observe the company's operations or talk to knowledgeable outsiders, then to come back with a written report. The purpose is to make the entire subject more significant in the employer's mind.

It is the same principle used by management consultants, advertising agencies, top sales producers and others when they want to stimulate a company to action.

The very act of a study, and the presentation of a report following it, builds an aura of importance. Your report doesn't need to be lengthy, and it doesn't have to require a great deal of work. It should, however, discuss the areas where you would hope to make significant contributions.

If you try the report option, be sure to stage it properly. Let the employer think it's important, and ask for adequate time to present your findings. Your report, of course, would include a recommendation that a job be created. If the report is well received, you will have succeeded in creating a job.

Chapter 8— Answering Ads

Ads are a longshot because everyone answers them and they are only 3% of the market. But, here are some tips that can help!

97% of all job openings are never advertised

❑ You need to start by recognizing that less than one in ten employers fills a single professional or managerial job through an ad over a 12-month period.

❑ What's more, many of the more attractive advertised openings bring 100, 200, or even 400 responses. Ads which attract up to 1,000 candidates are not that unusual. This clearly makes answering ads the most competitive area you can tackle.

❑ When you start your search, answer all good ads from the last 13 weeks. In some fields, the openings you uncover this way can be quite large. This is especially true as you go for higher income jobs.

❑ As you identify new advertisements to answer, delay your response five days, to minimize the risk of not making the first cut. When employers have to screen a lot of applicants, they begin by discarding resumes that include anything that will rule the person out.

❑ By the way, did you ever see an ad and feel "that describes me exactly"? Well, if you were a good fit for the job, answering ads twice can work. Very few of your competitors will do this, and employers give a big edge to people who really want to be with them.

❑ Since most resumes provide more facts, they can work against you in some situations. Make use of strong letters, ones that play back the requirements for success in the position. Whatever your basis for selecting an advertisement, in your letter be sure to let the employer know just why you selected it.

❑ If you see an ad you really like, try getting added information beyond what was in the ad. Then, use it in your response. Demonstrating industry knowledge works better than anything else.

❑ You might also consider making contact with employees in the company before responding, particularly those who are easiest to befriend: sales and marketing managers, public relations staffers, etc.

❑ The most important point we can make about answering ads is to make sure that answering ads gets less than 10% of your job hunting efforts! To enjoy great success at marketing yourself, you need to be creative, get out of your routine and start using other avenues.

Chapter 9— Resumes

Without the right resumes and letters you could job hunt forever. Here's what works in today's new market!

Most people cannot succeed with old approaches to resumes

With the explosion in the number of personal computers, many people now distribute resumes in very big numbers.

What does this mean for you? Well, the number of resumes circulated relative to the number of attractive professional jobs available is going up, and will continue to go up.

Hundreds of people are apt to answer every good ad. As many as 40,000 resumes arrive each month at offices of some of the major executive search firms. In short, the competition is intense. Even with a strong economy, the competition will continue to increase throughout the rest of the 90s.

Now, when you look for a job you are reduced to how you look on paper. *Fortunately for you*, over 95% of all resumes are far less effective than they should be. They are average in appearance, disclose too many liabilities, and are rarely interesting or imaginative. Just make sure that your resume does not fall into the same category!

We believe in narrative resumes that are written in a style that is similar to a letter. The first reason we prefer a narrative is because it seems like less of a sales pitch. If you scream a bunch of facts, you will never tell a persuasive story. What's more, narratives seem more personal, more dignified and more professional.

A narrative also enables you to avoid disclosing any liabilities. Besides, it enables you to write a "solution resume," one that crafts the best story for your needs. And, if there is a second career goal, it is easy to slant it into a second resume. In addition, once you have written a narrative, it's easy to adapt to your letters.

Narratives work best for all situations. These include when your resume is used as a leave-behind; when it is given at the beginning of an interview; when it is provided for contacts to distribute; and when it is sent out cold — and really has to perform.

"Why don't you just pick out the resume that looks the best?"

Here is an easy system for drafting superior narrative resumes

Your starting point is to select the resume format which offers the best way for arranging your background. There are four standard resume formats: the historical format, the situation format, the achievement format, and the functional format.

Your choice will depend on which assets or skills you wish to emphasize and which liabilities you need to downplay.

❑ The historical format outlines your career in chronological order. It works best for people whose careers include increasingly responsible positions.

❑ The situation format tells a story, giving fast moving explanations of situations and how you dealt with them, and can be good for generalists.

❑ The achievement format is often used by people when their main accomplishments may not be in their most recent position.

❑ Functional resumes portray your career according to business functions or skill areas, and are especially good for career changers.

Once you've decided on a format, you can lay out the framework for your resume. This means putting the headings and subheadings in place. Regardless of the format you've selected, your resume should normally include your objective, a summary of your main selling points, and a strong reinforcing description of your experience and accomplishments.

Next, put your objective at the top of your resume. This tells the reader that you are a person with clear purpose, and it enables an employer to quickly assess you in terms of positions that may be available.

Your objective should appear at the top of page one — immediately after your name and address. You may choose to focus on one or more titles or functions.

Regardless of your choice, they should relate to jobs that really exist. For example, "Controller... Assistant Controller," or you may choose to communicate functions if that is more suitable, e.g., "Production Control."

For persons with broader objectives a short paragraph may be used. For example, "Qualified as VP of Manufacturing for a medium sized firm or Director of Operations at a large firm."

Or, use a broad functional umbrella with a variety of alternative assignments suggested to a potential employer. For example: *advertising / sales promotion / public relations.*

Immediately following your objective, provide a brief summary of your most important qualifications. Many of the people who are going to receive your resume will initially glance at it for less than twenty seconds. That's why you need a summary of your most attractive assets to appear early in your resume.

This section may emphasize positive information on any aspect of your story, although most people will want to describe only work experience, education and their most important personal assets. Having an objective and a summary will help ensure that your main selling points will almost always be read. For example:

General Manager—
International Operations

Broad experience in international operations, both in large corporations and in start-up situations. Over the past ten years, I have traveled to most world capitals developing client relationships, negotiating acquisitions and making strategic trade decisions involving hundreds of millions of dollars.

My educational background includes an MS in Management Science from the University of Chicago plus a BA degree from Denison. Fluent in German, French and English. Married with two children.

When it comes to writing the copy for the main body of your resume, be sure to personalize your writing with a conversational tone. For credibility, describe your product, industry and market knowledge.

List positions you held with a given employer — as long as your titles show a pattern of advancement. With average titles use an upgraded term to reference them, e.g. "office management" instead of "administrative assistant." Recent experience is what counts.

If you have a long list of jobs, trim or combine the list and emphasize only the key situations. Share credit for larger achievements when you have played a role in the overall effort.

Make yourself appear as interesting as possible and build a positive bridge by surfacing a common interest. Mention sports, travel or military experience, clubs, awards, and hobbies.

List all degrees, as well as educational credentials that are pending. Include training through military schools, company-sponsored courses, seminars or evening courses. For recent graduates, good grades, part-time work, elected offices, sports, awards, fraternity or sorority involvements, and leadership can all help.

By the way— letters often work better than resumes

Custom marketing letters produce more interviews than sending resumes with cover letters. Sometimes people spot a fact in a resume and prejudge you. We have found there are ten letters you may need, and the more targeted your letters, the better your results.

Letters For Answering Ads

Letters For HR Executives

Letters For CEOs & COOs

Letters For References

Letters For Networking

Letters For Influentials

Letters For Following Up

Third Party Letters

Letters For Spot Opportunities

Letters For Recruiters

Mr. Robert Smith
Boyden Associates
123 E. 64th Street
New York, NY 10012

Dear Mr. Smith:

In the course of your search assignments you may have a requirement for an accomplished technical executive.

As a registered professional engineer with a B.S.E.E., my career has covered responsible positions with three blue chip firms: Ward Corp., Western Industries, and Pepsi.

As a consultant for Arthur D. Little, I have worked closely with the officers of many other major corporations focusing on a wide range of engineering problems. Advanced problem-solving in electronics is my specialty.

My ability to develop and implement solutions has brought praise from virtually all of my clients and saved them significant time and tens of millions of dollars.

Among my references are leading decision makers, presidents, and CEOs with Fortune 500 organizations.

The enclosed biography briefly outlines my experience over the past 17 years. My salary requirements are flexible, depending upon location and other factors.

Sincerely,

Tom Sands

Chapter 10— Interviewing

Our key to turning interviews into offers is to be able to build personal chemistry— fast!

Success depends 70% on your presentation and 30% on background

About 70% of your job hunting success will depend on your marketing and interviewing skill. What's more, the key to becoming great at interviewing is to know how to build personal chemistry.

Some people think interviews are just conversations, and others believe they are just sessions during which they have to answer questions. These things may happen, but an interview that turns into an offer involves far more.

Think about this. Last year there were more than 200 million interviews, and no two were the same. So how do you prepare? You do it the same way you would for a sports contest. There were millions of them and none were the same.

In an interview or a sports contest, you can't plan precisely how things will go, but you can have a game plan. That means knowing the points you want to touch on and the pace you want to maintain.

Interviewing, of course, is a selling situation. It involves the exchange of information and the building of personal chemistry. Naturally, it's not only what you say that's important. Let's look now at the key things you can do to build a positive personal chemistry.

Research can help build chemistry

Did you ever meet anyone who knew a lot about you? It takes you by surprise, doesn't it? It's a great way to make a positive first impression.

Many people have built successful businesses that way. One friend of mine, a consultant with a six-figure income, attributes his entire success to the research he does ahead of time.

Four out of every five of his clients tell him that he wins their business because he knows a lot more about them than anyone else. So make it your business to know as much as you can about the company, the industry, and if possible, about the person you'll be meeting.

Build chemistry
with the front office staff

Can you guess what percentage of executives say their secretaries' opinions influence them? What do you think? One-third? Half? Well, about two-thirds of them do.

Here's how this might affect you. Not too long ago, I was interrupted by Hattie, who stated that Mr. Baxter had arrived for his 2:00 interview. I had forgotten about the appointment and it was a busy day. I immediately asked, "What do you think of him, Hattie?" She didn't say a word. She just gave a thumbs-down signal.

That was the end for poor Baxter. No one ever taught him how important it is to make a positive impression with the front office staff. I told Hattie to have him see one of my assistants and to tell him her opinion first.

So, be attentive to the secretary and others who work up front. Remember, you can do more than make friends. Have a conversation that gives you information that will help in the interview. If you have to wait, and the secretary is too busy to talk, give the impression that you can put the waiting time to good use.

You may find, as many people have, that when you go out of your way to be respectful to them, they will often go out of their way to help you.

Build chemistry with your attitude and image

Psychologists tell us that the way we expect to be treated has a lot to do with the way we are treated. So build positive expectations and picture a friendly interviewer.

What determines this personal chemistry? People silently react to the image you project, your posture and body language, the things you say about any subject at all, and the way you answer questions. For example, each of us is continually projecting some kind of image. It isn't just physical image or dress either, although your appearance speaks before you say a word. It's also a matter of attitude, interest and enthusiasm.

Check out your image. Go to someone who is not close to you and ask what kind of an attitude they think you project. Get their honest opinion of your appearance, eye contact and mannerisms. Listen to what they have to say, then do the same thing with someone on your side. Somewhere between the two, there will be an accurate picture, and if anything needs to be worked on, do it.

Build chemistry by paying sincere compliments

Do people like receiving compliments? You bet they do. So, before the interview, read or talk to people about the company and uncover some good things to say. Somewhere in those first few minutes, find the opportunity to let the interviewer know that you heard good things.

This will accomplish the following. It will show that you know something about the company, and it's also what we call a "third-party compliment," where you are passing on the good news that you heard from others. Now, you can compliment their facilities, people, products, advertising, public relations or anything else. However, whatever you do, be specific.

Don't just say that people you know are impressed by the product. Talk about why they are impressed. Maybe it's that new product they added this year, or the designs they've adapted. Or maybe it's the reliability of their products.

All of us like to hear about how our products have pleased customers. By giving details, you show that you have given it some thought and that your compliment is not just empty flattery.

Listen, find out what they want
and build chemistry as you do it

How do you find out what the employer really wants? Just let your listening ability go to work. However, be ready to ask job-related questions that will start the person talking about the areas in which you can help the firm. One of the easiest ways to impress people is to ask intelligent questions about the firm and the job.

Find out what happened to the last person in the job. Ask the interviewer about his interests and experiences and that of his superiors. If a situation stalls, raise questions about any subject by asking who? what? when? where? and why?

Find out who the job reports to and how long they have been in it. Pinpoint the authority that goes with the job, and find out what they expect you to accomplish in the first six months. Ask a simple question such as, *"What would be the biggest challenge I would face?"*

Of most importance, find out how the interviewer sees the problem and what their expectations are. When you do this, you're learning what the unwritten requirements of the job are.

Chapter 11 — Negotiating

Most people find it awkward to negotiate. Our system uses a soft sell approach that always works!

This process is about the art of soft selling

There have been many books written by people who call themselves experts in negotiations, but they emphasize situations where you negotiate with someone you will never deal with again.

However, in the job search situation, the use of intimidation and attack strategies has no value. Techniques for one-upmanship can cost you the job. Here you're setting the tone for your long term relationship.

Never allow yourself to be seen as overly aggressive. In fact, the reason most people don't like the term "negotiation" is that they associate it with confrontation, being tough and role playing, something that does not come naturally.

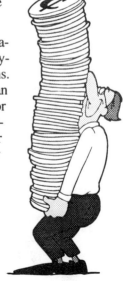

The truth is, the best negotiators are low-key. They avoid anything that might cause irritations. So remember, never project an image of being argumentative or emotional. Follow the best negotiators and make sure you appear sincere and reasonable— never cold or calculating.

Start negotiating only
after the employer is sold on you

Never attempt to negotiate until the employer is sold on you. Many people misunderstand and think of negotiation as selling. In truth, you cannot negotiate unless there is some hope that you can get the employer to offer new terms, and there is almost no chance they would offer you new terms unless they were sold on you.

When you are ready to negotiate, you will find it helpful to have clear ideas about what you want. Realizing that you will not achieve everything, keep your main objectives in mind, and do not risk an entire negotiation by coming on too strong about less important points.

Support what you want with only one or two strong reasons, rather than many which may be strong or weak. The moment you give a weak reason, the employer can use that as an excuse for not granting the item in question.

Never be afraid
to ask for what you want

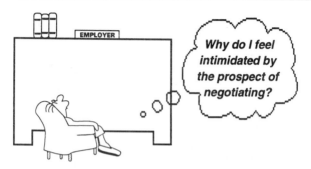

No one will ever withdraw an offer because you ask for something more. Always sell "quality" rather than "low starting price." After all, the easier you are to get, the less you'll be valued later on. If you are looking to change for a financial reason, don't appear greedy, but looking for a 15% to 30% increase is acceptable.

The salary for most jobs is usually flexible within a range. When an employer is willing to create a new position to bring you aboard, that's always your best opportunity for negotiating something attractive! Focus on negotiating a percent increase, as it is usually better to speak in terms of "percentages" instead of "thousands of dollars." It sounds like less.

Express some vulnerability to gain sympathy

Expressing a slight amount of vulnerability can be a very effective weapon in your negotiation process. It is done simply by letting the employer know that accepting the job on the terms offered would cause you some personal difficulties.

This plays to the employer's desire to make sure you are happy, so you can devote your full energies to the job. For example, you can be flattered by the offer, but you can say that you may have to sacrifice your current life-style in order to afford to take the job. And, of course, this would disappoint your family.

"I love the job and really want to join with you, but we'd have difficulty making ends meet. Is there a chance you could go a little higher?"

Question—
rather than demand

The best negotiators persuade others through questions. This gives them the information they need to put themselves in control of the situation. It also gives them time to think and never has them putting all their cards on the table.

For instance, good negotiators will not say, *"I do not agree with you because..."* Rather, they will say, *"Frank, you do make a good point, but I wonder if there is room for another point of view..."* or *"I accept that point of view, but it raises a question about..."*

They would never say, *"That would not be any good for me."* Instead, they might say, *"Bill, could you tell me how you think this would work for me?"*

Then, they will follow up with questions, so the employer can discover for himself that the proposal is not quite good enough. And that is your goal: to let the company discover for themselves the validity of your request.

They might never be persuaded if you tell them their point of view is wrong, but if your questions lead them to discover it, they will be much more disposed to changing the terms. So remember, question— do not demand.

Negotiate the nature
of the job and the responsibilities

If you can reshape the job into a larger one, the salary range will be higher.

How much responsibility can I negotiate... Sales Rep? Manager? or VP?

Start with positive comments about the job and the firm and suggest that they might benefit by adding responsibilities to the job. Then offer to share your thoughts on what might be added.

For example, *"Tom, there is no doubt that this is a good job. However, based on what you have told me, I believe I could be even more helpful if a few related elements were added. There are three areas where my experience could make a big difference."*

If the interviewer agrees these are important, have them added to the job description. Believe it or not, reshaping the job can often be just that simple!

Avoid discussing money until the time is right

Premature discussions about money or benefits can be a real deal breaker. Besides, the more enthusiastic an employer becomes about you— the more likely he'll be willing to pay more.

Sometimes an interviewer will begin with a statement like this: *"Jim, before we get started, I need to know how much money you are looking for."* The principle to keep in mind here is that you do not have to answer the question! For example,

"Bill, frankly, I could talk more intelligently about my circumstances after I know a bit more about the responsibilities and the growth that's possible. "

Or... *"Bill, I appreciate your being direct. I would not take your time if I did not have a fairly good idea of the range you would be willing to pay. If we can agree that my experience fits your needs, I doubt we will have a problem on compensation."*

Before the interview, figure out how you would handle the situation. If all else fails, give a range which surrounds your best estimate of the upper end of what the job might pay.

Be sure to never say "yes" or "no" immediately

If you are offered a job, but the salary is too low, let the employer know how pleased you are they made an offer. Take the opportunity to praise the firm and explain that you need some time to consider it.

"John, I am pleased you made me an offer. This is an outstanding firm, and the opportunity is excellent. I am sure you can appreciate that I would like some time to give it further consideration. May I get back to you tomorrow?"

When you call back, consider raising the possibility of redefining the job.

"John, as I said earlier, the idea of joining your firm is exciting. I want the job, but I have difficulty with the level of starting salary.

With children about to enter college, I had done some planning based on an income that was $5,000 higher. As I thought about that, however, I realized that jobs are not cast in bronze and that a company can often redefine a position to fit the talents of the person they want. Would it be possible to take another look at the job specs?"

For my part, I know that if you could make a modest additional investment, I would show you a handsome return through my performance. I sincerely want to work for you and hope that we can make some adjustment. Can we take a look at it?"

Of course, there may be situations where you do not want to redefine the job, but you would still like to raise the salary. Use the same technique, but show some vulnerability, then suggest that a specific dollar figure be added to the base salary. If that figure is within 10% to 15% of what you have been offered, the employer will not take offense and will grant you at least a part of it.

The reason for the positive statement is to reassure the employer that you think the offer is fair. Asking for more money is a negative, and it needs to be balanced by positives.

Use your enthusiasm as your major negotiating technique

If you load a maximum amount of enthusiasm into your statements, it becomes nearly impossible for the employer to conclude that you should not be with them.

To get an offer raised, consider the principle of introducing other criteria on which to base the offer.

This can include the following:

❏ The importance of the job to the firm,

❏ The value of your total package,

❏ What you believe the market is for persons with your background, or

❏ Other offers you are considering.

In the example that follows, notice how there are no demands, only questions. By your inviting employers to explore the situation with you, they are free to reach their own conclusions about whether their offer is too low. Using this approach, you come across as easy-going, sincere and slightly vulnerable, never as cold, calculating or aggressively demanding— never as someone who is putting them in a corner.

Chapter 12—Unemployment

If you become unemployed, here are the eight key steps you need to take.

Approach success as being inevitable. Your positive attitude can help you do it sooner rather than later.

Virtually everyone who becomes unemployed becomes re-employed. However, some do it quickly and successfully while others struggle, give up on themselves and settle for poor positions.

Today, unemployment is looked at from a far different perspective than in years past. For the most part, someone who becomes unemployed is viewed as a victim of economics beyond anyone's control.

Nevertheless, for those who lose their jobs, there can be a feeling of shock, disbelief and even fear. It can mean the loss of many symbols of security that we often take for granted. When we have a job, we have a place to go, an opportunity to achieve, tasks to fill our work day and people to work with, including close friends.

Even in cases where people resign, their initial feelings of self-confidence can quickly be lost if they don't land a new job quickly. Obviously, loss of income can also cause great apprehension.

Other people may not admit it and may be quick to claim they quit all their previous positions, but it is likely that many executives who will interview you will have shared the same experience at some stage in their career.

Being fired doesn't mean failure in the eyes of everyone else, even though you may feel tremendously depressed. Being unemployed does mean that you will be carrying a handicap, but don't feel sorry for yourself.

The eight key steps you need to take

■ Register for unemployment. Never let your pride stand in the way of accepting a weekly check.

■ Don't vacation. Start your campaign immediately, exercise regularly and be as active as you can.

■ Get access to an office phone. It helps to have a base of operations at an office. You might be able to use the number of a friend who can have his secretary take messages for you, or list a phone number (separate from your home phone) under your own consulting service. At the very least, establish a work station in your home, and let everyone know it is to be treated as your office.

■ Get yourself a mentor. You will need someone who is a source of encouragement and who can be a good sounding board. It can be a relative, friend or associate whom you respect. Share your progress with that person and maintain communication throughout the campaign.

■ Get support from your employer. In addition to outplacement assistance, they might provide office and secretarial help. Get total agreement on the reason for your separation. If there were negatives involved, work out an explanation which puts you in a fair light. Look for clarification that the termination was due to factors beyond your control, such as a reorganization. Get agreement that you had been a valuable contributor, and where it applies, that the final separation was arrived at jointly. Explain that you did not want to look for a job or take a lesser position while drawing a paycheck.

As far as your relationships with your most recent employer is concerned, don't imply threats. If you are in a position to harm your employer, they will know about it without your saying so; and they'll be taking it into account in dealing with you.

■ Invest in your campaign. If you lose your job, start investing in your campaign right away. See if your past employer will pay for outplacement. The effort will cost nothing, and if the answer is no, you haven't lost anything.

You should also complete a financial plan which assumes that you may be unemployed for the next six months. In the course of planning, make sure you eliminate all unnecessary entertainment and household luxuries. However, allow sufficient funds to enable you to dress well, to get any professional help you need, and to actively pursue a first-class job campaign.

■ Don't be overanxious. Never beg for a position and never try to explain your present situation in print. Everyone likes to hire talent that is hard to find. Don't show up in advance of your scheduled interviews, or be available at the first suggested time for further interviews.

■ Be as active as you can. Many people who have not been active have found that the more time passed, the less capable they were— psychologically and emotionally— to go out and do what must be done to win their new jobs.

The best psychological boost you can get will come from having a schedule of full activity: breakfast meetings, lunches, interviews, letter writing, phone calls, and follow-ups. The way to do that is to get into action and give your job search top priority. This is no time to start fixing up the house! Develop a discipline just as if you were going to work. Here's a brief list of other helpful hints for the unemployed.

Don't fail to accept introductions. Most people like to help their friends. Give them the opportunity!

Don't be unwilling to relocate. Sometimes it's better to go where the action is, and most people can adjust far better than they realize.

Don't feel sorry for yourself. You'll end up being the only one hurt by these emotions.

Be willing to consider a career or industry change. If your present occupation or industry is on the decline — now is a good time to make your move.

Don't allow your health to slip. Attitude and physical fitness go hand in hand.

If you need more help...
here's what Princeton/Masters
can do for you

■ Marketing assistance for helping
people— from $25,000 to $300,000 +

■ Affordable and tax deductible

■ Brings people more speed, convenience
and job hunting effectiveness

How we can help you anywhere in the U.S.

We work with employers and individuals in career transition in all 50 states. Our most popular program is available through any of our offices, and has been used by thousands of people on a long distance basis as well.

Here's how it works. We start by sending you a handsome binder containing our step-by-step system for finding the right new job. *(The book you have in your hand is just the tip of the iceberg as far as this material is concerned.)*

The information comes in eight easy-to-use sections, and is illustrated and in color. Six cassettes are also included—with help for special situations.

The pages that follow outline the benefits of this material and the invaluable reports which you can automatically order along with it.

1 Making you more marketable and raising your income potential

The package you receive includes our *Career History and Marketability Profile* which was mentioned on page 15. It will uncover every conceivable asset or skill that might enhance your marketability.

In addition, it gives you all the key phrases and concepts that employers seek in people they recruit. All you need to do is check the ones that apply to you, and incorporate them in your resumes and letters, and all other communications.

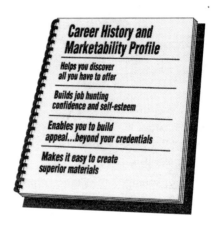

Career History and Marketability Profile

Helps you discover
all you have to offer

Builds job hunting
confidence and self-esteem

Enables you to build
appeal...beyond your credentials

Makes it easy to create
superior materials

2 Giving you the right contacts

Our research staff tracks special events that may signal the availability of unadvertised openings, and we provide a comprehensive report for metropolitan areas where we maintain an office.

Since you need to get your credentials to recruiters, we also supply a custom report on the recruiters who should receive a copy of your resume.

In addition, we also use the finest employer databases to give you the contacts you need. Princeton/Masters maintains *"more information" on "more employers"* than any other career firm in the U.S. We use this information to provide you with the right employer contacts in the industries and geographic areas of your choice.

These reports can be shipped in 48 hours

An extensive report on news events that may be leads to unadvertised openings

A report on all the recruiters that should be sent a resume

An in-depth report on employers to consider contacting by industry and area

From Princeton/Masters

Emerging Opportunities in the Metro Area

Firms with:
- Higher Sales and Profits
- Recent Expansions
- New Leases
- New Plants

From Princeton/Masters

Recruiters to Contact

- Company Name
- Address
- Phone Numbers
- Specialties

From Princeton/Masters

Employers to Contact in the Metro Area

- Names & CEO's
- Addresses
- Lines of Business
- Sales and Profits
- Numbers of Employees
- Phone Numbers

3 Giving you more career options

You will clearly be more marketable if you have more *"career and industry options."* The package we supply will introduce you to all of the country's hottest career fields and fastest growing industries.

In addition, once you complete a unique questionnaire that comes with the material, we prepare a *"Personal Profile Report"* to help you better select the career situation that's right for you. Thousands of people have praised the help these profile reports have provided.

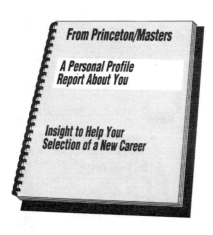

4 Giving you an action plan for getting interviews with more speed

If you use a "hit-or-miss" approach, you may never get introduced to enough good situations. The material you receive gives you all the latest insider techniques for the 90s, and gives you a complete marketing action plan to follow. It tells you precisely "*what*" to do and "*how*" to do it.

"The marketing plan in the Princeton/Masters Program gives you a step-by-step track for getting interviews. It can cut job-hunting time in half – and sometimes much more. Most important, people can get a lot more interviews in less time."

5 Giving you professional resumes & letters

The material we supply contains a full range of outstanding resume and letter samples, proven materials that have worked for others and which can do the same thing for you. They are very easy to adapt.

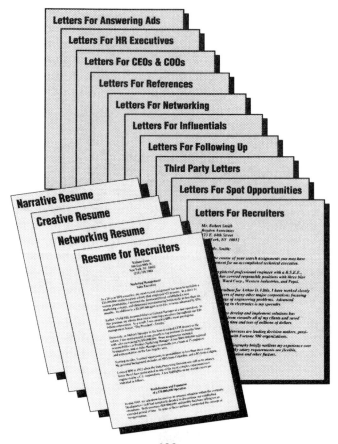

6 Building your interviewing and negotiating skills

You will also receive all the types of interview questions you might be asked, along with suggested answers to give and much more.

In addition, you will receive our full negotiation system, including information on everything you might be able to negotiate. Everything we provide is designed to build your self-esteem and make sure you are at your very best in all your interviews.

Finding the right new job can be your key to everything else in life.

Other help that can be made available

❏ <u>Professional resume writing services</u>

❏ <u>Distribution of your credentials</u>
We can prepare mailings to employers and recruiters as selected from our databases. This can be a great convenience.

❏ <u>Private instruction on the program</u>

❏ <u>Course instruction on the program</u>

What clients say about help from Princeton/Masters

Princeton/Masters has assisted thousands of men and women in all career fields and at all income levels. Here is a small sampling of comments that are representative of people's experiences:

"Thanks for the excellent help. By applying the Princeton/Masters system I landed my 'dream job' in less a month." **J.C.—Financial Executive**

"Please accept my heartfelt thanks for the positive impact you have brought to my life. I have accepted an attractive offer in sales management."

G.F.—Sales

"Your assistance was the total key to helping me secure my new position in less than 2 months. The Program is very well conceived."

R.M.—Engineer

"I have just accepted a new position in Materials Management. Your company serves a vital role for which all of your staff should be proud."

T.—Distribution

"Your program was in-depth and informative, and quickly implemented. I highly recommend it."
A.L.—Human Resources

"I accepted the position of President at a leading publishing firm. You were instrumental. Thanks again." **W.H.—President**

"I'm writing because I recently received an offer from IBM as a Vice President. Your resumes and databases really made the difference."

M.M.—VP Operations

"This is to let you know that I have received 7 offers of new employment. "   **B.D.—VP Sales**

"I am absolutely thrilled with my new marketing role with Coca-Cola. The program was excellent."

J.J.—Administrative Executive

"Every aspect of your marketing program was useful and my confidence was greatly expanded."

K.H.—Data Processing

"I received a signing bonus and a $15,000 higher starting salary. Your interviewing and negotiating system was the key for me."   **L.H.—R & D Director**

"Your program was a tremendous help. I was hired at Nordstrom's as a Senior Merchandiser. Your resumes, interviewing formula and strategies gave me the confidence I needed."

A.B.—Merchandiser

"Let me take the time to praise your program. Without it, I couldn't have received a high-level position."   **J.C.—Consultant**

Here's how you can take advantage of Princeton/Masters

To see how we can help you, please call either *Peter Bennett* or *Pat McDonald* of our national account service group at (800) 772-4446. They will be happy to send you free literature or answer any questions you may have. We also have offices throughout the United States and can refer you to our staff in your area.

Princeton/Masters International

7951 E. Maplewood, Ste. 333
Englewood, Colorado 80111